GOD'S Rx For A Hurting Heart

MARILYN HICKEY

Marilyn Hickey Ministries
P.O. Box 17340
Denver, CO 80217

Unless otherwise indicated,
all Scripture quotations are taken from
the *King James Version* of the Bible.

Printed in the United States of America
Copyright © 1984 by Marilyn Hickey
All Rights Reserved

CONTENTS

1. GOD'S Rx FOR HURTING HEARTS..............................7

2. MYRRH: THE SMELL OF TRIUMPH!!...23

3. MYRRH: YOUR WEAPON OF WARFARE...37

4. NAME YOUR DAY (THIRTY DAYS TO A HEALED HEART)...........................45
   Thirty Days of Devotions..48

5. CONFESS THE WORD FOR A HEALED HEART.................................91

6. MEET THE GREAT PHYSICIAN.........................95

1

GOD'S R_x
FOR HURTING HEARTS

God has an anointed prescription for hurting hearts, and it is guaranteed to work!!! Everyone has experienced hurts, sorrows, disappointments, and failures, but isn't it just like God to have one old-fashioned, heaven-sent remedy which will heal them all! He is so efficient, and His apothecary is absolutely within everyone's price range: It is FREE! His remedy is all-inclusive; it covers every imaginable pain. It doesn't taste bitter; it tastes sweet, and by taking it you will "fulfill all your days" and increase your life span!

Well, is your curiosity aroused? Do you want to know what it is? It is MYRRH, a beautiful aromatic spice with healing properties. I am going to show you where to find it and how and when to apply it. Get prepared to receive a BUNDLE OF BLESSINGS!!!

At the very beginning of His ministry, Jesus prophesied the end result of His mission by reading from the Book of Isaiah:

"The spirit of the Lord God is upon me; because the Lord hath anointed me to preach good tidings unto the meek; he hath sent me to bind up the brokenhearted, to proclaim liberty to the captives, and the opening of the prison to them that are bound; to proclaim the acceptable year of the Lord, and the day of vengeance of our God; to comfort all that mourn; to appoint unto them that mourn in Zion, to give unto them beauty for ashes, the oil of joy for mourning, the garment of praise for the spirit of heaviness; that they might be called trees of righteousness, the planting of the Lord, that he might be glorified" (Isaiah 61:1-3).

Is there anyone whom this prophecy doesn't cover?

What do the brokenhearted, the captives, the imprisoned, and the mournful have in common? They all have deep hurts within their hearts which are in need of healing. Isn't it wonderful that from the very beginning of His ministry, the Spirit of the Lord was upon Jesus with a special anointing to heal the hurting and the brokenhearted?

Have you ever had an emotional hurt? Well, God has a special anointing specifically designed to heal your heart when it hurts. Sometimes we mistakenly look to other Christians or to our mates when we are hurting, but often they are not as sensitive to us as we need them to be. Actually I think that their insensitivity can work for our good, because it will make us look to the only One to Whom we should turn: Jesus! Through Jesus we can draw upon that anointing of healing which God planned for us to have.

Where are we supposed to go in order to learn where to find healing after our hearts have been wounded or broken? When we're in a state like this, we need love. Did you know that there is a beautiful love story in the Bible that is full of illustrations of perfect love? That love story is the "Song of Solomon." The "Song of Solomon" had always been a puzzling book to me until the Lord gave me a simple key, which unlocked the whole book. We have to see the book written as a bridegroom speaking to his bride! I had always read it and interpreted it in the light of seeing Jesus as my Savior, but God said, "Don't read it like that! Instead of looking at Me as your Savior, look at Me as your BRIDEGROOM. Then you will understand what I am saying to you."

> "A bundle of myrrh is my well-beloved unto me; he shall lie all night betwixt my breasts" (Song of Solomon 1:13).

"Breasts" in this particular Scripture is sometimes translated "heart." This passage is saying that Jesus, my Well-Beloved, is myrrh to me, and He is lying upon my heart.

I knew that I had to discover the spiritual significance of myrrh and the similarities between myrrh and "my Well-Beloved." What is myrrh? It's a with a beautiful, aromatic fragrance. It can come in the form of sticks, crushed leaves, or oil. In order to discover the significance of myrrh, I began to look in Genesis, and my search took me through Revelation!

I found that myrrh is very expensive. When Jacob's sons had to go into Egypt to get food, Jacob wanted to send Pharaoh an appropriate present. He chose myrrh, because it was very costly. This illustration shows that when we begin to look at myrrh as a healing substance for the heart, we must realize that it is very, very expensive. It cost Jesus His life to heal your broken heart.

There are all kinds of hurting hearts: Someone is hurt because he has been rejected by a mate; someone else is hurt because he has had an emotional crisis in his childhood and has never been set free from the pain; another is hurt because of a set-back in a career or the death of a loved one. Hurts come in a variety of shapes and sizes, but remember that Jesus is the precious, expensive Balm that heals broken hearts.

In the Old Testament, I found that the sacrifices offered by the priests were mingled with myrrh. This was done to make the sacrifice have a sweet aroma. Can you imagine the smell of animals burning on the brazen altar? They burned the entire animal. The priests sprinkled the anointing oil, which was composed of a combination of myrrh and other aromatic spices, on the sacrifice for the purpose of making it smell more pleasant as it was burning.

Have you ever known that you had to make a sacrifice, and it really hurt? Jesus can show you how to make your sacrifices smell good. He will touch your heart, and whatever you have to give up will seem to amount to nothing.

I had the opportunity to apply myrrh to a very dear sacrifice during the early days of my marriage. As a young bride, I had always wanted a home. Both Wally and I realized the importance of acquiring our first home as soon as possible, and we purchased it just as soon as we were financially able. Prior to marrying Wally, I had a sneaking suspicion that he might be called into the ministry, and I realized there were very few young couples in the ministry who were able to afford their own homes. Before I married my husband, I told him "If you are considering the ministry, I will never marry you." "Oh, I'm not called into the ministry," he reassured me. And do you know what he did? He trapped me. After we were married, he was suddenly called into the ministry, and we had to give up our home. Oh, that hurt me so much! It was such a sacrifice for me. I moaned and groaned and griped and grumbled.

Then one day, the Lord just touched my heart, and it was as though that house meant nothing to me. By that time, we were in the ministry as traveling evangelists, and He put myrrh on my sacrifice, and it smelled **so** good to me. What's a house? I didn't even want a house for a while.

Another characteristic of myrrh is that it is a preservative. When they took the body of Jesus down from the cross, they anointed His body and His burial clothes with myrrh. They wanted to take advantage of the natural preservative qualities of this spice.

If you don't get emotional and heart wounds healed, you can actually shorten your life span. Did you know that people die of broken hearts? But the healing myrrh of Jesus upon your heart will preserve you from a premature death, physical distress, and many things which can hurt you and make you physically sick all your life. Some people are always sick because they are wounded emotionally. Jesus is myrrh to them, if they'll only turn to Him. He is a preservative to keep you from having a short life span.

Myrrh is also used as a disinfectant. I had to laugh about this, because my mother told me that when she was a little girl, her mother would put a little bag of camphor around her neck to keep her from getting colds. It was a kind of disinfectant. I thought, "Jesus is a bundle of Myrrh to us, and when we wear Him on our hearts, He keeps us from catching hurts and wounds." Some people are offended at every little thing. If you don't look at them in just the right way, they become all uptight, and you have to ask them, "What's the matter....NOW?" I have noticed that if I keep Jesus and the sweetness of His myrrh upon my heart, I'm not as easily offended nor am I so sensitive to the hurts which come my direction.

Queen Esther used myrrh to make herself beautiful (Esther 2:12). Myrrh upon your heart, a healed heart, a whole heart, is very beautiful. Do you know what people see? They see Jesus on your heart. People who do not have wounded spirits and are not always uptight about something have a lovely fragrance about their person. I don't believe that myrrh just beautifies and perfumes the outside of an individual. The myrrh of Jesus on your heart will radiate from the inside of your being to the outer man. Jesus is Myrrh, and He desires to make you beautiful!

Did you know that prior to going in before King Ahasuerus, Esther had to go through a ritual of purification for one year? During six months of the year, she was anointed with the oil of myrrh. This spice not only purified her, it covered her with a rich fragrance, and made her very beautiful. Can you imagine how beautiful you would look if you held Jesus on your heart and allowed His Word to purify you for six months?

Hegai, the king's Chamberlain, the keeper of women, was responsible for giving each woman who had an audience with the king, **anything** which they thought would make them more beautiful. When it was Esther's turn to go in before the king, she asked for nothing; rather, she relied upon Hegai's judgement. Undoubtably, Hegai had faithfully served the king for years, and he was well aware of his tastes. Just as Hegai carefully chose the things which would make Esther beautiful and find favour in the sight of the king, Jesus Christ will do the same for you. If you put His rich anointing of myrrh upon your heart, a supernatural beauty will radiate from your inner being, and you will find favour with both God and man.

Priests were also anointed with myrrh. When they prepared to go into the temple for their priestly ministry, they anointed themselves with a special oil, and part of it had myrrh in it. We are kings and priests, and we are sent to heal the brokenhearted. We're anointed with myrrh so we can be priests to people and minister to their broken hearts. I just love that!

One time when I was in the Chicago airport, a woman beside me was crying; she was very distressed and disturbed. Not long before my flight, she tapped me on the shoulder and asked for an aspirin. I told her that I didn't have any but she would be able to get one from the stewardess on her flight. I asked her if she was sick, and because I was concerned, I asked if there was anything I could do.

She said, "I'm in terrible trouble, and I saw you reading your Bible." (You should carry your Bible everywhere; it opens doors for ministering.) "I wondered if you are Orthodox," she said. "What's Orthodox?" I questioned. "I'm Russian Orthodox," she said, "and I believe that Jesus is the Way to the Father." I replied, "If that is the definition, then I'm Orthodox."

She then told me that her husband had highjacked a plane in the United States and that he was in prison. She had come from Paris to visit him. "We're in trouble, and he's a political prisoner," she said. I knew it was all true. She said, "I don't know what we're going to do, and I thought that since you have a Bible, you could possibly help me." I prayed, "Lord, how am I going to heal this woman? How am I going to help her?"

They were calling my flight, and I didn't know what to do. Instantly, the Lord showed me the most unique thing to do. He said, "Just take her into your arms and hold her. My love will continue to flow from Me into you, and it will flow from you into her." Praise God! That was wonderful! I will never forget it as long as I live! We're anointed to be priests. You have a healing anointing of myrrh residing in you as a believer: use it!

The priests also used myrrh when they

prayed. Myrrh was placed on the altar of incense and as they prayed, their prayers would rise up to the Father as a sweet smelling savor, and He would take delight in them. When we pray and intercede for the brokenhearted, I believe that an anointed fragrance of myrrh rises to the Father, He takes delight in our sacrifices of prayer, and He heals our loved ones. Psalm 141:2 says, "Let my prayer be set forth before thee as incense; and the lifting up of my hands as the evening sacrifice."

I thought about Jesus and looked at the times He was involved with myrrh. At His birth, the wise men brought gifts to Him, gifts of gold, frankincense, and myrrh. Gold is for a king, and Jesus is a King; frankincense is for a prophet, and Jesus is a Prophet; myrrh is for a priest, and Jesus is our "Great High Priest," and "He ever lives to make intercession for us." The myrrh was specifically brought for His anointing as a priest.

When Jesus was on the cross, we again see myrrh involved in His life. Myrrh has an anesthetic effect, and it deadens pain. Mark 15:23 tells us:

> "And they gave him to drink wine mingled with myrrh: but

he received it not."

Why didn't He take it? Wouldn't you have taken it? If He had taken that wine, it would have deadened His pain. Instead, Jesus said, "I won't take any pain medication; I want to take all the pain of the cross so I can deaden yours." That's why He refused myrrh.

Here is an interesting side thought which will bless you. "New Wine" is symbolic of the Holy Spirit, and often in Scripture, we see wine as a symbol of the blood of Jesus Christ. God the Father has mingled the myrrh of Jesus Christ with the "New Wine" of the Holy Spirit together with the cleansing power of the blood of Jesus Christ. Because Jesus refused to partake of the earthly counterpart of wine and myrrh when He was on the cross, the Father graciously allows us to partake of the heavenly counterpart: the "New Wine" of the Spirit which has been lovingly mingled with the healing myrrh of Jesus Christ and the cleansing power of His blood. PRAISE GOD! Isn't that beautiful! The "New Wine" of the Spirit and the blood and myrrh of Jesus will anesthetize, cleanse, and deaden every one of our hurts and pains.

There are times when our hurts are so very deep that simply deadening the pain of them and allowing them to heal naturally is not enough. In the Song of Solomon, it says, "a bundle of myrrh is my well-beloved unto me." He isn't just a little bottle of oil, nor a few crushed leaves; He's a whole bundle. At times, you need a bundle, because sometimes you have a bundle of hurts. He provided a stick of myrrh for each one of your hurts. He is not only a Pain Killer to the hurting heart, He is the Healer of your hurting heart.

When He died, they wrapped His body in spices, one of which was myrrh. When He was born, He was given myrrh; on the cross He was offered myrrh; and in His death He was anointed with myrrh. Why was He wrapped in myrrh at this time? Because myrrh has a very sweet smell, and Psalm 45:8 says,

> "All thy garments smell of myrrh, and aloes, and cassia, out of the ivory palaces, whereby they have made thee glad."

Other than being resurrected, this was one of the very last prophecies Jesus had to fulfill.

Jesus smells like myrrh; He smells so

good! Why? Because He smells like healing. He smells as though He is everything I need. He is that beautiful, satisfying smell; the fragrance which makes our hearts glad. Let's look again at the Song of Solomon; it tells us **when** we are healed, "my well-beloved is a bundle of myrrh to me; He shall lie all **night** upon my heart."

There is also a beautiful verse in Psalms which ties in with the same thought.

> "...He gives to His beloved even in his sleep" (Psalm 127:2b — NAS).

Did you know that even while you are asleep Jesus is healing you? He wants you to be whole and at peace **all** the time. If you've been hurt and are out-of-it, tonight just go to sleep in Jesus. Allow that precious myrrh of Jesus to deaden and take away all the awful pain you've been bearing.

When you let Jesus heal these wounds, when you let His myrrh heal you, you begin to smell like He smells. Then you won't need to go around saying, "If you'd been through what I've been through... ." Have you ever been around people who have been through a trial and are still hurting from it? When the three Hebrew children came out of the fire, they didn't even smell like smoke! When you've been with Jesus, you smell great. He always smells good, but some of us come out of trials, and **DO WE SMELL LIKE SMOKE!** We still gripe and groan. If you'll take a little myrrh, you'll stop griping and groaning, and you'll smell like Jesus. You won't smell of smoke! He will heal your broken heart.

2

MYRRH: THE SMELL OF TRIUMPH!

Remember the time when Moses and the children of Israel were getting ready to leave Egypt? The experience there had been a very bitter one for them, a very difficult time. Before they left Egypt, God commanded them to hold the first Passover meal. During this meal, which was symbolic of salvation, they ate bitter herbs along with the Passover lamb. You need to take your bitter herbs, your bitter experiences, and try them with Lamb. It's simply delicious!

They ate only a few bitter herbs, but they ate a whole lot of Lamb! The children of Israel walked out of Egypt so healed of everything that their feet didn't swell, and they weren't sick. God took away disease from their midst, and for 40 years they were well! That's the biggest healing service I've ever heard about!

There were three million people healed in one night, because they ate LAMB with their bitter herbs. They said, "Yes, we've been hurt, but we're taking the Lamb with us." If you'll take the Lamb with your bitter experiences, you'll walk out of them without any hurts on your heart; you'll emerge from them completely whole. People will notice and tell you that there is something about you that smells so good (because you've taken Lamb with your bitter experiences.) You'll just say, "It's just Jesus; I smell like Him."

Do you smell like Him? Have you ever wondered if others pick up the scent of "the savor of His knowledge" when they are around you?

"Now thanks be unto God, which always causeth us to triumph in Christ, and maketh **manifest the savour of his knowledge by us** in every place (II Corinthians 2:14).

Did you know that the Lord always wants you to triumph in Him? When you win, you smell good because you smell like a winner. You smell like you are healed. You smell like myrrh, because that is the way Jesus smells. He is the Pain Killer, and His sweet aroma spreads around. Why do some Christians smell bad? Because their hearts haven't been healed. It isn't because they don't use Right Guard. Most of them take baths and showers, but they don't get their hurt hearts healed; they don't manifest the savor of His knowledge! Instead, they moan and groan and are out-of-it. They never choose to walk into the realm of triumphant power, which is the "savor of His knowledge." They still hurt, because they openly refuse the remedy He has given for hurting hearts.

Would you like to be healed right now of a hurting heart? Some of you have had hurting hearts for a long time and have never before realized that Jesus can be your pain killer and your healer. Put your hand on your heart and pray:

> "Dear Father, in the Name of Jesus, I receive the healing, the myrrh of Jesus, into my broken heart right now. This moment, Jesus, my Well-Beloved, delivers me from this pain. He takes this pain and pours His myrrh into my broken heart. I believe that my heart is being healed right now, in Jesus' Name. Amen."

One time, I was very hurt by a situation

and circumstance. Years ago, a man who had been a friend of ours held a revival for us. He was young and single at the time, and we just loved him. My husband especially felt very close to him. One night, during a revival, the young man said, "Tomorrow night I will tell about the qualities I am seeking in the woman I will marry." Wouldn't you know, the next night the first three rows were jammed with young, single girls; they all brought pen and paper and took notes.

This is what he said he wanted: "I want a girl who can cook perfectly; she must be a marvelous gourmet cook. I also want her to sew so well that she can tailor clothes for me. In addition to being a candidate for Good Housekeeping's "Housekeeper of the Year Award," I want her to be beautiful. I don't want her to sing, play the piano or organ, teach Sunday School, or teach children. She is to have no ministry except me. I'm her ministry." I was amused and thought, "We'll see."

About a year went by, and my husband went through a very difficult experience in the ministry. If a difficulty were to arise now, we would know better how to claim healing and move in faith, but at that time we weren't as experienced. Wally told me one time, "I feel as though I have no one to whom I can go, who would really pray and minister to me. I feel that if I were to go to any of our people, they would put me down." Now that was a lie of the devil, because we have gone to them since, and they put us up, not down. They minister to us beautifully. Anyway, that is what the devil told him, and I agreed. (That is an example of the **POWER OF AGREEMENT** in reverse!)

He said, "I'm going to call this young man, because he's coming through Denver with his new bride; I'll ask him if he will just pray for me." The young man came to Denver and spent an afternoon with Wally. Then he came and talked with me. He said, "I found out what is wrong with Wally; I have the key!" "What is it?" I anxiously asked. He said, "It's you!" "Me!" I exclaimed.

No one could have hit me in a more vulnerable place. Absolutely nothing could have hurt me more than that remark. I asked, "Well, what is it?" "It's your ministry," he replied. At that time, I was doing practically nothing compared to now. I taught Sunday School, had a

Denver radio broadcast, and was on educational TV — that's all. "You shouldn't be in the ministry," he said. "you should just stay at home, cook, sew, wash and clean, and do NOTHING else."

I asked him what he thought I should give up? "Radio, TV, and your Sunday School class," he said. "You shouldn't do anything but wait on your husband. This is the source of your husband's problem, and he is hurting from it." The things this young man said hurt me, because my husband had always encouraged me more than anyone else and supported me in my ministry. I had always been shy and timid, but he pushed me out to minister; he had been so positive with me. I just didn't understand what this young man was saying. It bothered me, because I thought my husband had been putting on a front all those years and that he had been lying to me. I thought, "If he's lied to me about this, I wonder what else he has lied to me about?" I was extremely disturbed and upset.

This hurt so much in my heart that I couldn't tell anyone. I couldn't even talk about it for weeks. Finally, I went to a friend. She said, "Marilyn, you shouldn't come to me. You should go to Wally first.

Go directly to him and ask him if this is true." I did just that, and do you know how he responded? He just laughed at me. He said, "Marilyn, that is the funniest thing I've ever heard. You know how I've always encouraged you. It's funny, but that is this young minister's problem. Don't you remember what he wanted in a wife? She has to be beautiful, able to cook, able to make suits for him, and she couldn't do **anything** in the ministry. Marilyn, that's **his** problem. It isn't my problem, and it never has been. I didn't share anything like that with him; he just took everything I said and put that meaning on it."

Then this is what I did with my hurting heart: I just substituted the bitterness which I had for my husband over to that young man, who thought he had discerned those things. That wasn't getting healed, was it? I still smelled bad!

This young minister finally married, and every time he came through town, I really checked his wife out. I asked her, "Do you cook? Do you sew? Do you make your husband's suits?" She said, "I'm learning." She was very beautiful. Do you know what I did? Every time I knew they were going to be in town, I did my best to be gone. Of course, my husband was the first to notice. I said, "Well, I just feel led to leave at that time." Wasn't that an awful response? That's not healing! I still smelled bad. I still had not taken the myrrh that my Well-Beloved is to me. I hadn't pulled out the stick that would heal me. I pulled out sticks of myrrh to heal other things, but I hadn't pulled out the one necessary to heal this particular hurt.

The young man went to teach in a Christian university, and he wrote to my husband. He was so thrilled about the job, because he was free on weekends, and in the summer he would be free to minister in other churches. "I've always wanted to teach in a school like this," he wrote. I noticed on the stationery that a woman's name was listed as the president, and that really pleased me! I thought, "You know what I could do? I could write and say, 'Well! How do you like working for a woman? Ha! Ha! Ha!'" But that wasn't healing either!

The Lord really knows how to deal with you. Not long after the young man's correspondence with my husband, I received a letter from the female president of his university, asking me to speak there. If I were to go, I wouldn't have to write to him; I could just ask him in person! (That's still not healing the hurting heart!) When I was on the plane, en route to this speaking engagement, the Lord dealt with me, and dealt with me, and dealt with me. Finally, I said, "Lord, I don't know what to do with this situation; I'm still hurting from it." He tenderly said to me, "You hurt because you've never let Me heal you. I'm your myrrh. Let the myrrh of My anointing go into your heart." I just took a little stick of myrrh and put it where I was hurting, and by the time I got off the plane, I was just fine!

I went to lunch with this couple after the service, and I had none of the ugly feelings I would have otherwise anticipated. I didn't want to tell him off; I didn't want to do anything but be sweet. Believe me, that was a new attitude for me! I had been healed because I had applied the healing myrrh of Jesus to my heart. As we sat at lunch that day, the young minister had to leave early, and his wife had a chance to open her heart to me. She said, "I feel that I have no one to talk to; my marriage is in trouble, and I'm not allowed to do anything. I can't teach

Sunday School; I can't sing or play the piano; I can't do anything but cook, sew, and clean. I'm not allowed to take a job outside my home, and I am virtually a prisoner in my own house. I just can't stand it any more!"

It was at that point that the Lord showed me a revelation about hurting hearts. He said, "Marilyn, I allowed someone to hurt your heart because I wanted you to experience an offense, for the purpose of seeing the need which exists in the life of the person offending you. After you recognize the need, you will know how to intercede in prayer for them. If you absorb an offense and let it hurt you, you will never enter into intercession for your offender's needs. Neither of you will profit from the experience. I allowed you to see this young minister's need, but you took the offense personally and got hurt by it. All along, I have wanted you to have faith for his marriage and his ministry. If you don't pray, intercede, and stand in the gap for him, he will lose his ministry, and his marriage will be broken. You were too busy pitying your little heart, when I really wanted to heal it and give **you** the burden of intercession for this young man. I want you to smell like myrrh to them now."

That day, during lunch, I got to minister to the young man's wife in a very beautiful way. This was strictly the work of the Holy Spirit. When I left that young couple, I knew God had healed their marriage. I also knew He had given me a new revelation: When your heart has been badly hurt by another, analyze the offender's need and INTERCEDE for him. Give God the opportunity to heal you both — that way you'll both smell good; you'll smell of His myrrh; you'll smell like Jesus.

The young minister's wife called me about three months after our visit and said, "My marriage has been changed and transformed. I'm now teaching children's church." (That was a big step for her!) They now pastor, and she has a very active part in their ministry.

Not too long ago, someone told me, "This young minister just raves about your ministry. He beats the drum for you all the time. Is he a special friend of yours?" "You don't know how special!" I thought. Do you see what happened? I had not only experienced the healing myrrh of Jesus on my heart; I had also experienced the myrrh that could come OUT of me. In Song of Solomon, we find a beautiful illustration of this:

> "I rose up to open to my beloved; and my hands dropped with myrrh, and my fingers with sweet smelling myrrh, upon the handles of the lock" (Song of Solomon 5:5).

Why did my hands have myrrh on them? Because I was close to Jesus, and His myrrh rubbed off on me. When the myrrh was placed as a little twig on my heart, it became a part of me and just entered into my spirit, my very being. After the myrrh had been absorbed into every fiber of my being, everything I touched smelled like Jesus. There was the miraculous anointing of myrrh on absolutely everything.

In the first Scripture we examined from the Song of Solomon (1:13), did you notice where the myrrh was found? It was found on the heart, not on the shoulder, and there is a very important reason for this. God never intended for you to carry the burden of a broken heart. He wants to see you completely healed. Don't carry myrrh on your shoulder, because it will be of little benefit to you there. Carry it on your heart! If you do, you will always feel the precious anointing of Jesus upon your heart, and He will heal any hurt you will ever encounter, if you will only let Him!

I learned something else in The Song of Solomon about healing a hurting heart:
"...his lips [are] like lilies,
dropping sweet smelling myrrh"
(Song of Solomon 5:13b).

During times of pressure, have you ever studied and meditated upon God's Word, and possibly were perplexed over how to handle a particular situation or circumstance? But suddenly, a Scripture just bounced off the page to you, zeroed in on you, and you were healed. Have you ever had this happen to you? I'm sure you have! "His **lips** dropped sweet smelling myrrh." His Word will stand out to you, to be myrrh for you, and the myrrh-filled words will heal you. Not only is **He** a bundle of myrrh upon your heart, **His Words** are myrrh to the brokenhearted. As we take His Word into situations where we are hurt, we become healed. As we carry His Word to others, they become healed, because we begin to use the same balm or ointment which He uses in our healing process. Aren't you glad that Jesus is sweet smelling myrrh?

3

MYRRH: YOUR WEAPON OF WARFARE!

Have you ever considered myrrh as one of your "weapons of warfare?" It is! Let me show you how. The apostle Paul talks about our weapons being powerful because they are not carnal but spiritual.

> "For the weapons of our warfare are not carnal, but mighty through God to the pulling down of strong holds; casting down imaginations, and every high thing that exalteth itself against the knowledge of God, and bringing into captivity every thought to the obedience of Christ" (II Corinthians 10:4,5).

Our weapons are spiritual, and they are so strong that they can destroy all the areas of fear and pain which are strongholds within our hearts and minds. It is in **your** power to take captive any thought that is contrary to the picture of the victorious person the Word proclaims you to be. That principle is wonderful, because when you begin to build a new, positive self-image, the Lord starts to heal you.

There have been strongholds where we have hurt and hurt, and after they become saturated with myrrh, the fortresses of Satan come down. Perhaps we've imagined that some people don't like us, or possibly we've envisioned fears that were absolutely ridiculous. Regardless of the nature of our negative thoughts, when Jesus brings healing, tormenting thoughts begin to disappear. Our thoughts begin to get in line with God's Word, which is the "Word of Faith" which says, "We can do all things through Christ and will always be triumphant in Him!"

I looked at the above verse one day as I was having a very disturbing thought. The devil had told me for many years that I would have a nervous breakdown. My father had had two of them, and everyone constantly reminded me, "You're just like your father." I can remember that in my middle thirties I would entertain this thought. It began to take the form of a vivid imagination. If you entertain wrong thoughts, pretty soon you'll imagine them coming to pass, and you'll convince yourself they actually will! We went through some difficult things, and I felt as though I was going to crack and have a mental breakdown.

Then one day, I was going down our basement steps, when the devil came on full blast and said, "Why don't you commit suicide?" I really felt as though I was going to do it, because the impulse was so strong and forceful. I cried out to God, "Father! Father! Help me! I'm just like my father, and I'm going to have a nervous breakdown right now!" He answered, "Yes, you are just like your Father. I'm your Father, and I **never** had a nervous breakdown. You won't have one either." Hallelujah! Praise the Lord. I didn't have one!

When I realized the impact of this identity with my heavenly Father, the stronghold of suicide was cast down. That very day, I changed my mental attitude from one of defeat to an attitude of victory — exactly what the Lord had intended! When the Lord spoke that to me, it was a thought — an impression upon my heart. "I'm your Father, and you won't have a nervous breakdown." Then it became an imagination. I saw myself as a very wise, strong woman. "Marilyn Hickey — she's really smart. She has the mind of Christ; He is made unto her wisdom. She has an anointing from the Holy One; she knows all things." I began to reinforce the image of myself as being very wise!

I shared this revelation with my husband, and he jokingly said, "I wish you'd imagine yourself taking better care of your checkbook!" Imagination became reality. Now I **am** wise! Now there is a stronghold of God's Word in my life. Now, if the devil would come around and try to tempt me, saying, "You're going to have a nervous breakdown," I would just laugh at him and say, "You stupid thing! Satan, you know that I know better than that! I have built a stronghold of God's Word in that weak area!" Why? Because Jesus healed me. He gave me a revelation of myrrh by changing my thought patterns. He healed my imagination!

Now I pull down strongholds and imaginations and every high thing that exalts itself against the knowledge of God, and I bring every thought into captivity to the obedience of Christ. I do not allow imaginations to put me in bondage to fear. Instead, I take fearful imaginations captive. I lock them up and throw away the key. Jesus healed me of fearful imaginations, and He will heal you, too!

There is another important verse which directly relates to the subjects of obedience and the pulling down of strongholds. We usually don't associate it or hear it taught with the verses studied in II Corinthians 10:4,5. Look at this next verse.

> "And having in a readiness to revenge all disobedience, when your obedience is fulfilled" (II Corinthians 10:6).

When you get your thought life in line with God's Word, your imagination comes into line with His Word. You also build up God's Word into strongholds inside of you, and you become obedient to the Word. After your "obedience is fulfilled," you can help others whose thought lives are out of line, those who have hurting hearts. You can help them bring their thought patterns into line, because you understand how to use the myrrh upon them that Jesus used upon you. It works.

I want an anointing to come upon you as a priest to heal broken hearts. Nothing is more important than being used of God to heal the brokenhearted. Almost everyone is hurting. Jesus said, "The Spirit of the Lord is upon me, because he hath anointed me to preach the gospel to the poor; he hath sent me to heal the brokenhearted...." (Luke 4:18). I have found that the anointing which rests upon Jesus rests upon His Body, and the Church is His Body. When that anointing hit His Head, it flowed down all over His Body, all the way down to His feet. We have an anointing to heal the brokenhearted, and that anointing covers our entire body. I want that anointing to be upon you. God will lead you to brokenhearted people, and He will also show you how to smell like myrrh to them. They will learn how to let Jesus rest upon their hearts and find out how He is their well-beloved. Are you ready? Pray this prayer:

> "Father, I come to You in Jesus' Name. He is real to me, because He is my great High Priest. He has healed my broken heart, and His

anointing rests upon me. I know that as a joint heir with Christ, the blessing of a double portion is mine. Right now, I ask for a double portion of His special anointing so that I, too, can heal the brokenhearted and set the captives free. Lead me to brokenhearted people, and let me set them free with the precious anointing of your Word. Let me smell like myrrh to them. When I am through, let them carry the sweet fragrance of myrrh, also. I pray this in Jesus' Name. Amen."

Will you take God's anointed prescription for a hurting heart? It was very costly for Him; He had to give up His Son, Jesus. He has graciously made it available to you at absolutely no cost. Can you afford to refuse it? Can you afford not to share it with others?

4

NAME YOUR DAY (THIRTY DAYS TO A HEALED HEART)

Every day I name my day with the Word and claim the particular blessings which I know that I will need for the day. Did you know that it's Scriptural to name things? God gave Adam the authority to name every living creature, and they responded to him by coming to him when he called them. God renamed Abraham and Sarah. "He called things that were not as though they were," and by doing so, Abraham and Sarah became the father and mother of many nations; their infertility was reversed!

I know that there are circumstances which you would like to see **reversed**, and I want to show you how to do it.

First, begin by naming each day and calling a healing to an area of your heart which is hurting. After 30 days, you will have had plenty of practice, and you can enthusiastically continue the process on your own. If you do this, believe that you'll see miraculous differences not only in your heart, but in your total outlook on life. You will understand the **authority** which is yours as a believer. I'm sure you realize that when Adam fell, he lost **all** of his authority because of his sin. Jesus, the second Adam, redeemed us from both the curse of the law and the curse of Adam's fall. We can now name things in authority, because Jesus regained this power for us.

By naming your day early in the morning, you will be doing three things:

1) You will create a vision in your spirit of the goal that you are planning to accomplish for the day. "Where there is no vision, the people perish..." (Proverbs 29:18). Don't perish! Choose life! Get a fresh vision for each new day.

2) You will change your thought life. Philippians 4:8 teaches us, "Finally, brethren, whatsoever things are true, whatsoever things are just, whatsoever things are pure, whatsoever things are lovely, whatsoever things are of good report; if there be any **virtue**, and if there be any praise, think on these things." Virtue means "life-giving substance." Concentrate on visions and thoughts

which will generate life. Bring your mind in line with the promises which God has for you. The Word says that "we are more than conquerors through him that loved us" (Romans 8:37). If the Word says you are a conqueror, then you are! **Think** like one, and you will **live** like one! You will set the life giving power of God's Word in motion for your life.

3) Stand on the promise that God will create the fruit of your lips as you name your day! Boldly speak forth the things that your heart desires as you name your day. Speak forth your healing. Several times during the day, remind yourself **out loud** what you have named your day. Find Scriptures which will reinforce your visions and goals for the day, and plant them in your heart by saying them.

Get excited! Start to activate God's promises today. Ignite the beginning of every day in a positive way: Name Your Day and expect to bring a healing to **every** area of your heart!

NAME YOUR DAY

Day One

Today I name my day GARMENT OF PRAISE DAY. I will put on the Garment of Praise and cast off the spirits of heaviness and depression.

Don't allow depression, heaviness, and problems to weigh upon your heart. Recognize Satan, "the spirit of heaviness," and bind him. Remember why Jesus came to earth: "To appoint unto them that mourn in Zion, to give unto them beauty for ashes, the oil of joy for mourning, the garment of praise for the spirit of heaviness; that they might be called trees of righteousness, the planting of the Lord, that he might be glorified" (Isaiah 61:3).

When you carry around heaviness, depression and despair, you are not acting like a tree of righteousness, and you're not bringing glory to the Lord. It hinders your productivity! It hinders your spiritual growth! It can stunt you as a Christian. You can be kept from being more than a conqueror. If you have wondered how to get rid of depression, this Scripture tells you what to do: you are to take the garment of PRAISE and **give Him** the spirit of heaviness.

Determine in your heart to praise God in all adverse circumstances. Instead of being covered with the ashes of despair, radiate His beauty! You're the Bride of Christ; put on your wedding garment of PRAISE!

Day Two

Today is the day that my HEART will soar like an eagle above circumstances, and I will be "...blessed...with ALL spiritual blessings in heavenly places in Christ" (Ephesians 1:3).

Have you noticed that whenever you are emotionally depressed, your entire body feels weak and lifeless? All energy appears to vanish. God's Word has a solution: you are to "**wait** upon the Lord."

Do you know what happens when you

"wait upon the Lord"? You have a glorious promise: "He giveth POWER to the faint; and to them that have no might he INCREASETH STRENGTH. Even the youths shall faint and be weary, and the young men shall utterly fall: but they that wait upon the Lord SHALL RENEW THEIR STRENGTH; they shall MOUNT UP with wings as eagles; they shall RUN, and not be weary; and they shall WALK, and not faint" (Isaiah 40:29-31).

Let the Lord renew your physical and emotional strength today! Mount up as an eagle over all your circumstances; the higher you get, the less significant your problems become. Be blessed today "in heavenly places in Christ Jesus!"

Day Three

Today is my WISDOM DAY! Sunesis WISDOM, found in the Word, is the wisdom to meet practical needs.

If you have been a Christian for any length of time, you have read, heard, and been involved with many of the promises in the Word. These Scriptures are stored in your spirit until a need in your life demands their application. This is shown in Psalm 51:6 — "Behold, thou desirest truth in the inward parts: and in the hidden part thou shalt make me to know wisdom."

Learn the Word, meditate upon the Word, and speak the Word. Bring the healing power of the Word deep into your heart, and you will gain "sunesis" WISDOM.

"Sunesis" wisdom combines the Word you have hidden in your heart with your problem or need, and shows you how to apply the promises found in God's Word. The Holy Spirit will quicken the Word to your heart, and the ability of that Word will transform your situation. Apply "sunesis" WISDOM to your heartaches today.

Day Four

Today I am filled with CONFIDENCE! I have CONFIDENCE that my mind and emotions are being totally healed!

Do you remember the token of God's

covenant to Noah? It was the rainbow, and it foreshadowed Jesus. Just as the rainbow covers all the colors in the spectrum, II Corinthian's 1:20 tells us that "all promises of God are yea (YES) in Christ." Noah gained his covenant through 120 years of persistence, and his life and the lives of his family were saved. Confidently determine in your heart to gain your covenant: all the promises in Christ. Don't despair! Don't give up! Every time you see a rainbow, let it remind you of all the promises you have in Christ. That thought alone should be a constant source of encouragement!

Be confident! If you let go of your confidence, you'll never see the rewards which God desires you to have. Hebrews 10:35 commands you to "Cast not away therefore your CONFIDENCE, which hath great recompence [promise] of reward." Envision a completely healed heart which is enlarged and filled with all the promises of God. Confidently decide you will receive all the promises which God's covenant has in store for you.

Day Five

Today I will be HEALED from the bruises of rejection!

Have you ever coped with rejection? People in counseling and psychiatric professions say that it is one of the more difficult problems for the human personality to handle. Rejection often leaves scars that are hidden deep within our emotions, and it can definitely mar our self-images if we allow it.

Today I want you to look at Jesus. He was a man who experienced extremely deep levels of rejection. In Isaiah 53:3, Jesus is described: "He is despised and rejected of men; a man of sorrows, and acquainted with grief: and we hid as it were our faces from him; he was despised, and we esteemed him not." Why did Jesus suffer the pain of rejection? He did it so that your heart wouldn't need to be in bondage to the **burden** and pain of rejection. Isaiah 53:4 says, "Surely he hath **borne** our griefs, and carried our sorrows... ." If you have been carrying around the sorrow of rejection, you've been carrying a burden which God never intended you to have. Don't allow Satan to defeat you with rejection; turn all of the scars, hurt, and pain over to Jesus and walk away from them.

Today praise and thank God that through Jesus Christ, all the grief of rejection has been carried away from you, and your heart is completely HEALED!

Day Six

Today I will REMEMBER THE GOODNESS OF GOD!

In Psalm 103, we see David reminding his soul to "bless the Lord" and remember all of His benefits, of which there were many: forgiveness, healing, redemption, satisfaction, and renewal.

God's court of law will "forgive all thine iniquities," God's hospital will "heal all thy diseases," and God's market will repurchase and "redeem thy soul from destruction." Enter God's throne room, and you will be "crowned with lovingkindness." Dine in God's banqueting hall, and He will "satisfy you with all good things." Go to God's fountain of youth and "your youth will be renewed like the eagles" (Psalm 103:5).

Purpose in your heart to REMEMBER GOD'S GOODNESS in every part of your life; make a firm resolution to FORGET all past pain, discomfort, and bitterness.

Day Seven

Today is my day of PEACE. I claim the PEACE of God that passes all understanding.

Fear is the opposite of peace. No one enjoys being frightened. In Hebrew, the word "baath" means to be "affrightened." Job poetically used this word to describe his grief after his great trials. The word "baath" conveys the meaning of desert winds, grievous visions, discomforting pain, and a panting heart.

God has freely given us a remedy for all the above calamities. Philippians 4:7 tells us that "the PEACE of God, which passeth all understanding, shall keep your hearts and minds through Christ Jesus." When you keep your mind on Jesus Christ, God's Incarnate Word, you will never be "affrightened;" you will remain in "perfect peace."

Concentrate today upon keeping your

mind focused upon Jesus. When you enter a difficulty, ask yourself, "How would Jesus handle this situation?" Do you remember what He said to the storm? He said, "Peace, be still." Do the same in all your difficult circumstances! Speak PEACE to them.

Day Eight

Today I am DELIVERED from bitterness and rebellion!

You can find how strongly God deals with rebellion by reading the Book of Deuteronomy. Rebellion is basically disobedience. This word has a bitter meaning, and it leads to a bitter end. Did you ever realize that a disobedient person could not even be buried with the faithful? To "disobey" also means to be "bitter." Resentment and bitterness, then, are considered by God to be the same as rebellion. That is pretty strong!

Bitterness **is** difficult to deal with, but nevertheless, we are exhorted to "Let all bitterness, and wrath, and anger, and clamour, and evil speaking, be put away from you, with all malice" (Ephesians

4:31). We are told to be "imitators of God," and we should do it by "being kind to one another, tender-hearted, forgiving each other, just as God in Christ also has forgiven us."

Don't allow the seed of bitterness to take root in your heart. A healed heart, a whole heart, is a heart free from all bitterness! Claim your DELIVERANCE today!

Day Nine

Today I will EMBRACE God's promises! My heart will take delight in every one of them.

Today make an effort to find several promises in the Word which apply to your situation and EMBRACE them. You might be asking, "Marilyn, how do I embrace a promise. What do you mean?" When you embrace a promise, you draw it into your heart. You enthusiastically greet it, salute it, and welcome it, saying, "This is mine!"

The more we embrace a promise, the more emphatically we can say, "This promise will come to pass in my life. I will not let it go!"

In the eleventh chapter of Hebrews, we see several instances of saints who embraced God's promises. They were people who held fast to God's promises, regardless of their circumstances. Do you remember what the Bible said of them? By faith they saw miracles: the walls of Jericho fell down, kingdoms were conquered, the mouths of lions were shut.

Those who embraced God's promises were **convinced** that His Word would bear fruit in their lives. What promises are you claiming for your heart? If you don't have any, find some and EMBRACE them today!

Day Ten

Today is my day to LOVE. I will LOVE with God's LOVE shed abroad in my heart by His Holy Spirit.

We will reap what we sow, and today I want you to decide to sow LOVE. In John 13:34, 35, Jesus said, "A new commandment I give unto you, that ye love one another; as I have loved you, that ye **also** love one another. By this shall all men know that ye are my disciples, if ye have love one to another."

The love we demonstrate for each other is infectious. Non-Christians will see it and want what we have — Jesus! Decide today to correct any differences that you may have with someone else. Go out of your way to walk "the extra mile" to love the person who has offended you. You will **not** be sorry. Why? Because you'll be acting like Jesus.

Remember: He loved us while we were yet in sin, and His love was so strong that He was willing to die for us. Because He first demonstrated His love towards us, we love Him. Purpose in your heart to SOW LOVE to someone who is particularly not expecting it. Surprise someone by showing them the LOVE OF JESUS today!

Day Eleven

Today I am filled with REVELATION. My heart will be strengthened by a fresh REVELATION of Jesus today!

Won't it be wonderful to see Jesus? The apostle John did! But in I John 1:1-4,

John tells us that he also "gazed" upon Him. What is the difference between gazing and seeing? In Greek, the verb "to see" is "horan," and it simply means "to see with physical sight." The verb "to gaze" is "theasthi," and it means "to gaze at someone or something until a long look has caused the person to grasp a REVELATION of the meaning and significance of a certain person or thing."

John learned how to gaze upon Jesus until he beheld His glory (John 1:14). John gave Jesus more than a passing glance; he looked steadfastly upon Him and discovered many dimensions of His grace, loveliness, and power.

Strengthen your heart. Take time to minister and look intently upon the face of Jesus. Discover a new REVELATION of Him! Gaze upon Him today through the Word.

Day Twelve

Today I will STAND IN THE GAP for someone I love. I will not allow Satan to bring fear and concern into my heart over that person's well-being.

In Ezekiel 13:5, God says, "Ye have not gone up into the gaps, neither made up the hedge for the house of Israel to stand in the battle in the day of the Lord." God is looking for people to stand and have their own hedges complete and to STAND IN THE GAP for others. Whenever a hedge is broken down, the enemy can come in and attack the weakest area. How do we stand in the gap for another? We pray in the Spirit for them and bind the power of the enemy! We tell him "Satan, you cannot come in and attack this area. I am standing in this weak area with the power of the Word of God, and I will stand here until this hedge is rebuilt!"

Many of you have experienced heartaches because of the actions of your loved ones. Perhaps you see them in sin and separated from God. Your heart doesn't need to carry this pain; the Lord has given you a solution: Stand in the gap for them until they are strong enough to build their own hedges. Find promises in the Word of God which cover their particular situation that you can speak over their weak areas. The weapons of your warfare are not carnal, but mighty through God to the pulling down of strongholds. Use your weapons of warfare; pray in the Spirit and pull down Satan's strongholds, in the lives of those you love. Don't allow Satan to fill your heart with fear when you think of them. Claim God's promises and STAND IN THE GAP for them.

Day Thirteen

Today is my day of COURAGE. I will not allow unseen fears to grip my heart.

When Jesus walked upon the water, the disciples were afraid because they thought He was a ghost. Jesus called to them and said, "Take COURAGE: it is I; be not afraid." Peter responded by saying, "Lord, if it be thou, bid me come unto thee on the water" (Matthew 14:28). Jesus said, "Come." Peter started to go to Jesus, but when he **saw** the boisterous wind, he began to sink.

But did he really see the wind? Probably not! It would have been possible for him to see the effect which the wind had upon the water, the ship, his clothes, etc., but he couldn't see the actual wind, which was invisible. Peter had started to sink because something that he couldn't see gripped his heart — it was fear.

Are unseen fears gripping **your** heart? If so, recognize them and bind them with the Word! Don't allow your fears to take form or substance. Don't think about them, and above all, don't speak them! We are commanded to be "casting down imaginations, and every high thing that exalteth itself against the knowledge of God, and bringing into captivity every thought to the obedience of Christ" (II Corinthians 10:5). What are we to think about? In Philippians 4:8, Paul said, "Finally, brethren, whatsoever things are true, whatsoever things are honest, whatsoever things are just, whatsoever things are pure, whatsoever things are lovely, whatsoever things are of good report; if there be any virtue, and if there be any praise, think on these things."

Take COURAGE! Fill your mind, heart, and spirit with the good things of God today.

Day Fourteen

Today is my day of OVERWHELMING VICTORY. "Thanks be unto God, who always causeth me to triumph in Christ..." (II Corinthians 2:14).

Nine years after David was anointed to be king, he was an outcast of Israel! He was living in a Philistine city, Ziklag, with several hundred of his men and their families. "Ziklag" means "overwhelming despair." What a place for the future king of Israel to live!

One day after returning home to Ziklag, David and his men found that all their wives, children, and possessions had been stolen by the Amalekites. David's men picked up stones to stone him. Instead of saying, "Go on and get it over with," David encouraged himself in the Lord. He convinced his men that they were capable of reclaiming their wives, children, and possessions from the hands of the Amalekites.

David and his men found the Amalekite camp and not only got back all of their wives, children, and possessions, they confiscated all that the Amalekites had as well. When David returned to Ziklag, it was no longer a place of overwhelming despair; it was a place of OVERWHELMING VICTORY. Shortly after returning to camp, men came to tell him that both Saul and Jonathan had been killed and that they wanted David to become king!

What would have happened if David had given up when his men wanted to kill him? He never would have received his promised reward! He would not have been made king. God has given you exceedingly great and precious promises, but if you give up before you receive them, you'll cut yourself off from a blessing. Hang on! You can do it!

If you have been living in Ziklag, a place of overwhelming despair, purpose in your heart to live in a place of OVERWHELMING VICTORY. Go out and reclaim the promises that Satan has stolen from you!

Day Fifteen

Today is my PROVISION day! My every need has already been provided through Almighty God, El Shaddai.

God first revealed His name, El Shaddai, (Almighty God) to Abraham, the "Father of Faith." "Shaddai" is sometimes translated "breast," and it reveals the dimension of God's nature which nourishes and supplies all PROVISIONS which "pertain to life and godliness" (2 Peter 1:3).

How does your heart need to be nourished? The Bible tells us to "desire the sincere milk of the Word." Do you know what the nourishment of God's Word will do in your heart? It will strengthen, build up, fortify and heal the weak and wounded areas of your heart.

El Shaddai abundantly provides for those whom He loves. Naomi, Ruth's mother-in-law, is an example of a woman who suffered heartaches due to the loss of her husband and two sons. She told her neighbors, "Do not call me Naomi, call me Mara, for the Almighty has dealt very bitterly with me" (Ruth 1:20). Her heart was wounded, but nevertheless, she referred to God as "El Shaddai," and He healed her grief. Her daughter-in-law, Ruth, married Boaz, and Naomi became a grandmother! Naomi's friends blessed her by saying, "May he [Obed, her grandson] also be to you a restorer of your life and a sustainer of your old age... ." (Ruth 4:15). The birth of Obed renewed joy in her heart and healed the pain of her bitterness.

Naomi recognized God as El Shaddai and He filled her heart with a love which she thought had been irretrievably lost. Know God in His fulness as El Shaddai! Call upon His name. Give Him the opportunity to touch your heart and emotions and heal them, just as He did the heart of Naomi.

Day Sixteen

Today I will STOMP OUT the memories of rejection in my heart, for I am in Christ and "He hath put **all** things under His feet" (I Cor. 15:27).

Did you know that Satan has been put under your feet? Are you aware that the pains and bruises associated with rejection have also been put under your feet? Romans 16:20 says, "And the God of peace shall bruise Satan under your feet shortly." Isn't that a wonderful promise? Because you are a joint-heir of Jesus Christ, Satan and every pain that he has ever brought against you are all under YOUR feet! Because you are **in** Jesus, you are meant to bruise Satan; he is not to bruise you.

Right now, I want you to think of some bruised or wounded area in your heart. I also want you to think of an area where you have experienced rejection. Today, you are going to take care of all of those memories once and for all! Place them under your feet. You are going to STOMP on them and proclaim this faith confession with me.

"I declare boldly that Satan will not continue to bruise me with memories of rejection. Satan and all of the pain of rejection are now under my feet, and I am stomping on them. I am now free, because Jesus has set me free. Praise the Lord!"

Day Seventeen

Today is my day of FULLNESS. The FULLNESS of the Godhead, Jesus Christ dwells in my heart, and I am complete in Him!

Do you know what living in God's FULLNESS means? 1 Peter 4:7, 8 gives you four requirements which are necessary if you are to live in His FULLNESS. Number one: Be steady in Mind; Number two: Be sober in mind; Number three: Preserve your prayer life; Number four: Cherish your Christian brothers. Don't let your heart be pulled every which way; keep it fixed upon the Word of God. Ignore sense knowledge and walk by faith and not by sight; if you do, you will be walking "sensibly," according to the Word. Pray in the Spirit; don't let go of your prayer life. Be filled with constant unfailing love for others; walk in the fullness of the love of Jesus Christ!

Examine your heart to see if you meet the requirements for living up to God's standards. The FULLNESS of the Godhead, Jesus Christ, is living in you to help you meet them and to conform you to His image. Jesus wants you to experience Him in all of His glory. Fill your heart with Him today!

Day Eighteen

Today is my GLORY day. Today the GLORY of the Lord my God shall be upon me, and He will establish the work of my hands (Psalm 90:17).

Psalms 89:17 tells us that God is the "glory of our strength." Do you know where this GLORY resides? It lives in your **heart**! When the Tabernacle in the wilderness was set up, it was set apart and anointed. The cloud of God's presence came down, filled the tent, and the glory of it was such that Moses couldn't enter it. Then God said, "My glory sanctifies this tent;" it was completely filled with the beauty of His strength and presence.

God's beauty and glory now resides in living, human tabernacles — the hearts of His children. His cloud of glory has come down and filled your heart; don't let any sin enter your tabernacle. Keep your heart full of the glory of God. Do you know what will happen as you hold His glory in your heart? Your heart will be healed and strengthened, and filled with the fulness of the Godhead, Jesus Christ; your heart will grow **in** Jesus "from glory to glory." Others will see the beauty of God's anointed presence resting upon you. Let the GLORY of Jesus Christ fill your heart today!

Day Nineteen

Today I have a NEW IMAGE. I will allow others to see the IMAGE of Jesus Christ in me.

Have you ever been concerned about your IMAGE? Well don't be! See yourself through God's eyes; He sees you as perfect, because He sees you in the completed image of His Son, Jesus. Colossians 3:10 says we have "put on the new man, which is renewed in knowledge after the image of Him that created him." The knowledge which renews us comes from the Word of God, and the Word is the mirror which reflects our new, beautiful image back to us. As we read the Word it renews our mind and shows us **who** we are **in** Christ. If we don't daily look into the mirror of God's Word, we can forget who we are and lose the image which God has of us. What is that image? The GLORIFIED image of Jesus Christ!

Today as you read the Word, put on your new man and walk in the image of Jesus Christ. Walk victoriously, triumphantly, and in the power of the Holy Spirit. Let others see the IMAGE of Jesus Christ in you today!

Day Twenty

Today the Lord will ESTABLISH my heart, and I know that it will not be moved. (Psalm 112:8)

Has your heart ever felt troubled or torn over difficult decisions? Perhaps you were so frustrated that you simply didn't know which way to turn. The Word has some very special promises that will ease your heart and bring it peace whenever you find yourself in such a predicament. Meditate upon the following Scriptures:

"Keep thy heart with all diligence; for out of it are the issues of life... Ponder the path of thy feet, and let all thy ways be **established**. Turn not to the right hand nor to the left; remove thy foot from evil" (Proverbs 4:23 and 26,27).

"He brought me up also out of an horrible pit, out of the miry clay, and set my feet upon a rock, and **established** my goings" (Psalm 40:2).

"Commit thy works unto the Lord, and thy thoughts shall be **established**" (Proverbs 16:3).

The Lord will establish your thoughts, and by doing so He will give you direction and show you the paths that He desires you to follow. Commit your heart to diligently following His word; don't turn away from it, neither to the right nor to the left, and He will ESTABLISH your heart in His peace!

Day Twenty-one

Today is my HEAVENSENT VISION day. I will delight myself in the Lord, and He will give me the desires of my heart! (Psalm 37:4)

Do you know what a HEAVENSENT VISION or dream is? Sometimes it can come to you in the night, but most often it will be a vision that you will see in the eye of your spirit. The Lord gives you the vision and will lead you toward specific goals which He wants you to accomplish. These dreams or visions can be in the form of intense desires. Psalm 37:4 tells us that if you will delight yourself in the Lord, He will give you the desires of your heart. He will not only place His dreams in your heart, He will SUPERNAT-

URALLY enable you to accomplish them.

God gave Abraham a desire for a child, but after the dream took root in his heart, God enlarged his friend, Abraham's expectations. He first promised Abraham that his seed would be as the "dust of the earth" (Genesis 13:16). Later He elevated the scope of Abraham's vision to the heavens, and God enlarged his dream by saying: "Look now toward heaven, and tell the stars if thou be able to number them: and He said, so shall thy seed be" (Genesis 15:5). What did Abraham see when he looked into the sky? He not only saw the stars that he could see with his naked eye, he saw countless stars in an infinite number of galaxies, for he knew that His God, El Shaddai could fulfill any dream, no matter how large!

Do you have a special dream or desire in your heart that you would like to see God bring to pass? A healed heart is one that is filled with God's visions and dreams. Forget past pain! "Delight yourself in the Lord and He **will** give you the desires of your heart!"

Day Twenty-two

Today is my INHERITANCE day, for I believe that the Lord will give me the heathen for my INHERITANCE.

Have you ever experienced heaviness in your heart because your loved ones did not know Jesus Christ? I'm sure that you have. Today, you are going to discover God's peace as it flows into this area of your heart. He has given us a very special promise not only for our loved ones, but also for those in distant parts of the world who do not know Jesus as their personal Savior. In Psalm 2:8 God says, "Ask of Me, and I shall give thee the heathen for thine inheritance, and the uttermost parts of the earth for thy possession."

I would like you to examine a very unusual verse found in Ezekiel 27:31: "And they shall weep for thee with bitterness of heart and bitter wailing." The Hebrew word for **weep** is "sapad," and it denotes smiting the breast, as in a gesture of mourning, especially for the dead. As children of the living God, we ought to mourn in prayer and intercession for those who are dead in their sins.

There is a desperate need for those who

will intercede for the lost. The Word emphatically promises that "the effectual **fervent** prayer of a righteous man **availeth** much" (James 5:16). Rest in this promise, knowing that as you fervently intercede for your loved ones, God will honor His Word and give you "the heathen for your INHERITANCE." Your heart does not need to be troubled over your loved ones: Claim His sweet blessing of peace!

Day Twenty-three

Today I will CAST all my cares on Him, for I know that HE cares for me.

Has your heart been carrying around unnecessary burdens and anxieties? I Timothy 1:1 tells us that Jesus Christ is our hope. If you are troubled by worries or fear, you should ask yourself the same question that David rebuked his burdened heart with in Psalm 43:5: "Why art thou cast down, oh my soul?" Don't be cast down and lose hope! Paul said that Jesus Christ is the "hope of **your** glory" (Col.1:27). Focus your thoughts upon Him, and He will keep your heart in "perfect peace."

Psalm 16:7-11 gives you a beautiful prescription showing how you can unburden your heart: "I will bless the Lord, who hath given me counsel: my reins also instruct me in the night seasons. I have set the Lord always before me: because He is at my right hand, I shall not be moved [troubled]. Therefore my heart is glad, and my glory rejoiceth: my flesh also shall rest in hope. For thou wilt not leave my soul in hell; neither wilt thou suffer thine Holy One to see corruption. Thou will show me the path of life: in thy presence is fullness of joy; at thy right hand there are pleasures for evermore."

Unburden your heart today: CAST ALL of your cares on Him!

Day Twenty-four

Today is my REVIVAL day! God will REVIVE my contrite and humble heart!

In Psalm 85:6, David said, "Wilt thou not revive us again: that thy people may rejoice in thee?" "Revive" means "to live again." Where do you rejoice? In your heart, of course. Allow God to bring His resurrection power into your heart to revive and restore the dead places. Your life may seem to be dead, but the Lord **will** revive you.

"To revive" also means "to recover from sickness," and it applies to all sicknesses: spiritual, emotional, mental, and physical. Whatever your need, allow the anointing power of the Holy Spirit to REVIVE you.

The visitation of the Lord's Spirit preserved Job. The reviving of God's Spirit will bring new life into every area of your being. Revival is the opposite of flat, dead, and stagnant. You can keep revival in your life through God's Word and stay renewed in your body, soul, and spirit.

Rejoice in your heart, for the Lord has promised: "For thus saith the high and lofty One that inhabiteth eternity, whose name is Holy; I dwell in the high and holy place, with him also that is of a contrite and humble spirit, to revive the spirit of the humble, and to revive the heart of the contrite ones" (Isaiah 57:15).

If you need forgiveness, seek it today, and God will REVIVE your heart!

Day Twenty-five

Today I will dwell in THE SECRET PLACE of the Most High. I will abide in the shadow of the Almighty.

I will say of the Lord, He is my refuge and my fortress: my God; in Him will I trust.

Surely He shall deliver me from the snare of the fowler, and from the noisome pestilence.

He shall cover me with His feathers, and under His wings shall I trust: His truth shall be my shield and buckler.

I shall not be afraid for the terror by night; nor for the arrow that flieth by day.

Nor for the pestilence that walketh in darkness; nor for the destruction that wasteth at noonday.

A thousand shall fall at my side, and ten thousand at my right hand; but it shall not come nigh me.

Only with my eyes shall I behold and see the reward of the wicked.

Because I have made the Lord, which is my refuge, even the Most High, my habitation; there shall no evil befall me, neither shall any plague come nigh my dwelling.

For He shall give His angels charge over me, to keep me in all my ways.

They shall bear me up in their hands, lest I dash my foot against a stone.

I shall tread upon the lion and adder: the young lion and the dragon shall I trample under foot.

Because I have set my love upon Him, therefore will He deliver me: He will set me on high, because I have known His name.

I shall call upon Him, and He will answer me: He will be with me in trouble; He will deliver me, and honour me.

With long life will He satisfy me, and show me His salvation. (Psalm 91)

Day Twenty-six

Today my future is SECURED! God is my eternal refuge. I know that my future is SECURE, and my heart has nothing to fear.

Have you ever felt insecure or afraid over your future? Has your heart been troubled over what your circumstances might be in two years? Ten years? Twenty years? Well, don't be! In

Deuteronomy 33:27, the Word promises: "The eternal God is thy refuge, and underneath are the **everlasting arms**: and he shall thrust out the enemy from before thee; and shall say, destroy them."

"Eternal" means "to go before" or "precede," as found in Psalm, 89:14: "Justice and judgment are the habitation of thy throne: mercy and truth shall go before thy face." Lastly, "eternal" means "to be in front." Psalm 139:5 says, "Thou hast beset me behind and before, and laid thine hand upon me."

God goes before us and behind us, and He is a canopy over us. Beneath us are His everlasting arms. He completely encircles us with His love. We are not to be concerned or afraid of the future, because He is our future! If we are in Him, our future is SECURE; no one can snatch us out of His hand! We are in His **eternal** care!

Day Twenty-seven

Today is my day of TRIUMPH! My heart is glad, because Jesus Christ causes me to TRIUMPH in **all** things.

In Roman triumphs, the victor came riding in with his victim chained to the wheels of his chariot. The burning of incense accompanied the procession. To the victim, this scent meant sure death, but to the victor the aroma meant rewards. In ministering the Gospel, there are no victims — only victors! "Minister" means "TO TRIUMPH," so we should carry the scent of victory everywhere we go.

II Corinthians 2:14,15 tells us how to revive a failing heart. "Now thanks be unto God, which always causeth us to triumph in Christ, and maketh manifest the savour of his knowledge by us in every place. For we are unto God a sweet savour of Christ, in them that are saved, and in them that perish." A triumphant feeling revives and renews a failing heart. Get excited! Minister the anointing love of Jesus to someone else's heart. Carry the scent (knowledge) of Jesus to someone else today!

Look at your own situation. In what area of your heart do you need to experience a triumphant victory? Bring the knowledge of Jesus, the Living Word, into your situation. Seek the Lord for His wisdom, and you will TRIUMPH in all areas of your life.

Day Twenty-eight

Today I am RESTING in the Lord. My heart will trust in Him and I'll not fear.

Did you know that Solmon wrote Psalm 127 just before the death of his father, David? Solomon's brother, Adonijah, was trying to take the throne by deceitful means, even though the kingship was promised to Solomon. Instead of fighting with Adonijah over the throne, Solomon wrote this Psalm. Basically, it says, "Why worry? If God wants me on the throne, I'll be there." His heart was at peace with the Lord.

Solomon had received a spiritual name from Nathan, the prophet. The name was Jedidah, which means "beloved." When Solomon wrote Psalm 127, he said, "He giveth his beloved sleep." Solomon was really inserting his own name, Jedidah. Read this Psalm, and you can insert your name, too, for you are dear to His heart: you are His beloved.

Can you take the step of faith that Solomon took? Can you look at your own situation and say, "Why worry? God's Word is true; He will perform that which He has promised!" Of course you can! As you go to sleep tonight, remind yourself of **who** He says that you are. "God calls things that are not as though they were," and He has given this awesome power to you! Once you speak His Word over your situation, the work is already accomplished, whether or not you see the work as completed with your natural eye. Let your heart REST in the assurance of His Word. Stop worrying, you are of His beloved; He has called you "Jedidah." You are His bride, His chosen, and you above all others should let your heart REST in Him.

Day Twenty-nine

Today I have MOUNTAIN MOVING FAITH. I believe that as I speak to the problems which have burdened my heart, they will be removed!

Do your prayers move mountains, mole hills, or nothing at all? Would you like to see the mountain of defeat, depression and heartache lifted? Today we will put an end to defeat; we will MOVE MOUNTAINS!

In Mark 11:23, Jesus taught, "For verily I say unto you, That whosoever shall say unto this mountain, Be thou removed, and be thou cast into the sea; and **shall not doubt in his heart**, but shall believe that those things which he saith shall come to pass; he shall have whatsoever he saith."

When was the last time you spoke to the mountains which have covered your heart? God didn't say, "Pray to Me and I will remove them." The Word commands **us** to speak to them and tell them what to do. What is bothering you? Right now, address the problem in the name of Jesus and tell it to be removed and cast into the sea. Whenever the problem tries to resurface, speak the Word against it and command it to be removed. Believe that what you say will come to pass; believe that your commands will move your mountains of problems and circumstances.

When you pray, don't pray the problem; pray the **answer** to the problem. Jesus said, "What things soever ye desire, when ye pray, believe that ye receive them, and ye shall have them"

(Mark 11:24). Pray the things which your heart **desires**. MOVE YOUR MOUNTAINS today, and call rivers of joy into your heart.

Day Thirty

Today is ABUNDANCE day. I believe that I will experience the true meaning of life and that I will have it more ABUNDANTLY.

Today I will show you what happens when the Holy Spirit "rains" in your heart. "The Word is Spirit, and it is life. As your heart hears the Word, the Word falls like rain upon your heart. It waters all the good things you have been sowing in your heart as you "Named Your Days" during the past month. The more you hear the Word, the more nourishment your crop will receive from the rain of the Holy Spirit.

Hosea 10:12 says that the Lord will "rain righteousness upon you." What is the typology of rain? Rain can mean a sprinkling, but it can also mean an outpouring. Rain is usually found to be a type of the Holy Spirit, whose wonderful outpouring we are expecting in ABUNDANCE. I Samuel 20:36 also speaks of a rain that "shoots as an arrow." If you'll be faithful to apply the Word of God to your life, that Word will pierce your heart as an arrow. The piercing of the Word won't hurt; it will heal your heart. As the rain comes down, what you have sown in your heart will grow, and you will yield an ABUNDANT harvest of the fruits of righteousness.

Day Thirty-one

This is the day I will turn curses into BLESSINGS. My heart will be healed of the negative things which have been said about me in the past!

Have you ever been discouraged because negative prophecies which people had spoken over you came true? Perhaps someone said, "You are always going to be fat; the women in your family have always been big-boned." Possibly people have inferred that they really don't expect very much out of you, and as a result you seldom exceed their expectations. Today is the day you will turn negative words (curses) into BLESSINGS! How will you do it? You will use the Word of God.

Make a list of the negative things that have been said in the past, which have cut deeply into your heart. Today you will be healed from this pain. Find promises in the Word of God which will transform your situation. For instance, if someone has said you are clumsy or bungling, proclaim, "I can do all things through Christ who strengthens me." In the face of talk about sickness, rebuke it by saying, "The joy of the Lord is my strength," or "Bless the Lord, O my soul, and forget not all His benefits: He forgives all my sins and heals all my diseases!"

After you find the promise which covers your situation, you must say it. Confirm it over and over. Each time that your heart is troubled by a painful memory, proclaim a BLESSING over it and rebuke the curse! Turn your curses into BLESSINGS today!

ARE YOU CONVINCED?

In the last thirty days God has anointed your heart as you have sown His Word into it, every day. You've planted incorruptible seed, and each day your heart has been encouraged, renewed and refreshed by the Word. By now I know that you are hooked on the habit of "naming" each day, because you've begun to see results not only in your life, but in the lives of others around you. I truly hope that "Naming Your Day" becomes a life-long habit.

Every day, expand the expectancies that you have planted in your heart by reinforcing them with the Word. I guarantee, you'll never be disappointed!

5

CONFESS THE WORD FOR A HEALED HEART

In addition to "naming" each day, it is necessary for you to continually feed your spirit with healing verses from the Word of God. Say the verses, memorize them, hide them away in your heart. Let them sink down deep into your spirit until they become a part of you. They'll not only bring healing to your heart, you'll always have them available to touch others with love and bring the healing Word of Jesus Christ to those who are in need.

"Though an host should encamp against me, my heart shall not fear..." (Psalm 27:3).

"The Lord is my strength and my shield; my heart trusted in him, and I am helped: therefore my heart greatly rejoiceth; and with my song will I praise him" (Psalm 28:7).

"I will wait on the Lord and be of good courage, and He shall strengthen my heart" (Psalm 27:14).

"My heart is fixed, O God, my heart is fixed: I will sing and give praise" (Psalm 57:7).

"Thy word have I hid in mine heart, that I might not sin against thee" (Psalm 119:11).

"I will run the way of thy commandments, when thou shalt enlarge my heart" (Psalm 119:32).

"I shall not be afraid of evil tidings: my heart is fixed, trusting in the Lord" (Psalm 112:7).

"I will trust in the Lord with all my heart; and lean not unto my own understanding. In all my ways I will acknowledge Him, and He shall direct my paths" (Proverbs 3:5,6).

"I will keep my heart with all diligence; for out of it are the issues of life" (Proverbs 4:23).

"A sound heart is the life of the flesh..." (Proverbs 14:30). I have a sound heart and good health in all my flesh.

"Thou hast put gladness in my heart, more than in the time that their corn and their wine increased" (Psalm 4:7).

"God hath also sealed me, and given the earnest of the Spirit in my heart" (II Corinthians 1:22).

"And the peace of God, which passeth all understanding, shall keep my heart and mind through Christ Jesus" (Philippians 4:7).

"The day star (Jesus) will arise in my heart" (II Peter 1:19).

6

MEET THE GREAT PHYSICIAN

There will be a few of you reading this book who have never received Jesus Christ into your hearts as your personal Lord and Savior. In order to receive the anointing which will heal your hurting heart, you must meet the Great Physician first! He is lovingly waiting for you to call upon Him to heal you of the pain and burden of your sins. The Bible says that "without shedding of blood is no forgiveness" (Hebrews 9:22). God the Father has provided an unblemished sacrifice for you, and it is the only sacrifice that is acceptable in His sight. The Lamb of God is His Son, Jesus Christ*, and His blood was shed as the perfect sacrifice for your sins. Receive the free gift of salvation today! Jesus is waiting to come into your heart and triumphantly enter it as the Great Physician and your Lord and Savior.

Don't hesitate! Pray this prayer right now!

>Dear Heavenly Father,
>Be merciful to me, a sinner, and forgive all my sins. I believe that Jesus Christ died for me and that He arose on the third day to give me eternal life. Cleanse me from my sin and guilt with His precious blood. I believe that from now on when You look upon me You will see me as spotless because I have been covered with the blood of Your Son, Jesus. Jesus, I now invite you into my heart to become the Lord of my life. Thank You for saving me.

Do you realize what has happened? You are "a new creature in Christ Jesus! Old things have passed away, and, all things have become new." Celebrate your new found joy and peace with someone you love. Share Jesus!

---

*In Hebrew, "Jesus Christ" is "Yeshua a' Messiah." If you are Jewish, take this opportunity to meet Yeshua, the Jewish Messiah. His blood was shed as the perfect sacrifice for your sins. He is the fulfillment of the promise found in Isaiah 53:5: "But he was wounded for our transgressions, he was bruised for our iniquities: the chastisement of our peace was upon him; and with his stripes we are healed." Call upon His name today! Accept Yeshua, the Jewish Messiah as your Lord and Savior.

Receive Jesus Christ as Lord and Savior of Your Life.

The Bible says, *"That if thou shalt confess with thy mouth the Lord Jesus, and shalt believe in thine heart that God raised him from the dead, thou shalt be saved. For with the heart man believeth unto righteousness; and with the mouth confession is made unto salvation"* (Romans 10:9,10).

To receive Jesus Christ as Lord and Savior of your life, sincerely pray this prayer from your heart:

Dear Jesus,

I believe that You died for me and that You rose again on the third day. I confess to You that I am a sinner and that I need Your love and forgiveness. Come into my life, forgive my sins, and give me eternal life. I confess You now as my Lord. Thank You for my salvation!

Signed_____Date ___ _____

Please print.

Name (Mr. & Mrs. / Mr. / Miss / Mrs.)_____

Address _____

City _____ State/Province _____

Zip/Postal Code _____

Country _____

Phone (H) ( ) _____

Write or call... We will send you information to help you with your new life in Christ: Marilyn Hickey Ministries • P.O. Box 17340 • Denver, CO 80217 • For prayer call: 303-796-1333. For product orders call TOLL-FREE at 888-637-4545. On the worldwide web at **www.mhmin.org**

TOUCHING YOU WITH THE LOVE OF JESUS!

Marilyn Hickey
PRAYER CENTER

When was the last time that you could say, "He touched me, right where I hurt"? No matter how serious the nature of your call, we're here to pray the Word and show you how to touch Jesus for real answers to real problems.

**Call us and let's
touch Jesus, together!**

303-796-1333

WE CARE!

Prayer Request(s)

Let us join our faith with yours for your prayer needs. Fill out the coupon below and send to Marilyn Hickey Ministries, P.O. Box 17340, Denver, CO 80217.

Prayer Request(s) _____

_____

_____

_____

_____

_____

_____

Mr. & Mrs.
Mr.
Name Miss
Mrs. _____ Please print.

Address _____

City _____ State/Province _____

Zip/Postal Code _____

Country _____

Phone (H) ( ) _____

If you want prayer immediately, call our Prayer Center at 303-796-1333, 24 hours a day.

WORD to the WORLD COLLEGE

Explore your options and increase your knowledge of the Word at this unique college of higher learning for men and women of faith. Word to the World College offers **on-campus and correspondence courses** that give you the opportunity to learn from Marilyn Hickey and other great Bible scholars. WWC can help prepare you to be an effective minister of the gospel. Classes are open to both full- and part-time students.

For more information, complete the coupon below and send it to:

**Word to the World College
P.O. Box 17340
Denver, CO 80217
303-770-0400**

Please print.

Name (Mr. & Mrs. / Mr. / Miss / Mrs.) _____

Address _____

City _____ State/Province _____

Zip/Postal Code _____

Country _____

Phone (H) ( ) _____

(W) ( ) _____

BOOKS BY MARILYN HICKEY

A Cry for Miracles	$7.95
Acts of the Holy Spirit	$7.95
Angels All Around	$7.95
Armageddon	$4.95
Ask Marilyn	$9.95
Be Healed	$9.95
Bible Encounter Classic Edition	$24.95
Book of Revelation Comic Book (The)	$3.00
Break the Generation Curse	$7.95
Break the Generation Curse–Part 2	$9.95
Building Blocks for Better Families	$4.95
Daily Devotional	$7.95
Dear Marilyn	$7.95
Devils, Demons, and Deliverance	$9.95
Divorce Is Not the Answer	$7.95
Freedom From Bondages	$7.95
Gift-Wrapped Fruit	$2.95
God's Covenant for Your Family	$7.95
God's Rx for a Hurting Heart	$4.95
Hebrew Honey	$14.95
How to Be a Mature Christian	$7.95
Know Your Ministry	$4.95
Maximize Your Day . . . God's Way	$7.95
Miracle Signs and Wonders	$24.95
Names of God (The)	$7.95
Nehemiah—Rebuilding the Broken Places in Your Life	$7.95
No. 1 Key to Success—Meditation (The)	$4.95
Proverbs Classic Library Edition	$24.95
Psalms Classic Library Edition	$24.95
Release the Power of the Blood Covenant	$4.95
Satan-Proof Your Home	$7.95
Signs in the Heavens	$7.95
Soul Food: Daily Nourishment from Psalm 119	$14.95
What Every Person Wants to Know About Prayer	$4.95
When Only a Miracle Will Do	$4.95
You Can! Bounce Back From Your Setback	$19.95
Your Miracle Source	$4.95
Your Total Health Handbook—Body • Soul • Spirit	$9.95

Prices are in U.S. dollars. If ordering in foreign currency, please calculate the current exchange rate.

Marilyn Hickey Ministries

Marilyn was a public school teacher when she met Wallace Hickey. After their marriage, Wally was called to the ministry and Marilyn began teaching home Bible studies.

The vision of Marilyn Hickey Ministries is to "cover the earth with the Word" (Isaiah 11:9). For more than 30 years Marilyn Hickey has dedicated herself to an anointed, unique, and distinguished ministry of reaching out to people—from all walks of life—who are hungry for God's Word and all that He has for them. Millions have witnessed and acclaimed the positive, personal impact she brings through fresh revelation knowledge that God has given her through His Word.

Marilyn and Wally adopted their son Michael; through a fulfilled prophecy they had their daughter Sarah, who with her husband Reece, is now part of the ministry.

Marilyn has been the invited guest of government leaders and heads of state from many nations of the world. She is considered by many to be one of today's greatest ambassadors of God's Good News to this dark and hurting generation.

The more Marilyn follows God's will for her life, the more God uses her to bring refreshing, renewal, and revival to the Body of Christ throughout the world. As His obedient servant, Marilyn desires to follow Him all the days of her life.

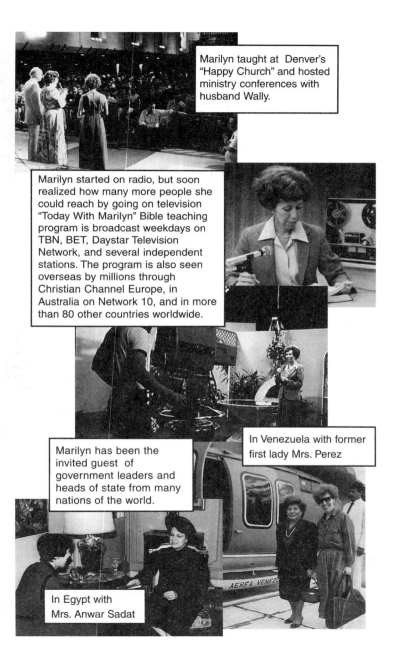

Marilyn taught at Denver's "Happy Church" and hosted ministry conferences with husband Wally.

Marilyn started on radio, but soon realized how many more people she could reach by going on television "Today With Marilyn" Bible teaching program is broadcast weekdays on TBN, BET, Daystar Television Network, and several independent stations. The program is also seen overseas by millions through Christian Channel Europe, in Australia on Network 10, and in more than 80 other countries worldwide.

Marilyn has been the invited guest of government leaders and heads of state from many nations of the world.

In Venezuela with former first lady Mrs. Perez

In Egypt with Mrs. Anwar Sadat

Marilyn speaks in Korea at Dr. Cho's church and is on the board of directors.

God has opened doors for the supplying of Bibles to many foreign lands—China, Israel, Poland, Ethiopia, Russia, Romania, and Ukraine, to name a few.

Marilyn and Sarah have a heart for China and for ministering overseas.

Food, Bibles, and water wells have been supplied to many countries, such as Haiti, the Philippines, Ethiopia, Honduras, India and El Salvador.

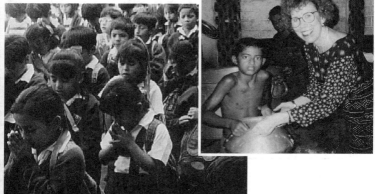

Marilyn and Sarah have ministered in many exciting areas such as Russia, Ukraine, Hong Kong, China and countries of Africa.

Marilyn has held Bible Encounters in Malaysia and Singapore.